FOR LISA

PUBLISHED BY DOUBLEDAY
a division of Bantam Doubleday Dell Publishing Group, Inc.
666 Fifth Avenue, New York, New York 10103
DOUBLEDAY
and the portrayal of an anchor with a dolphin
are trademarks of Doubleday,
a division of Bantam Doubleday Dell Publishing Group, Inc.

Library of Congress Cataloging-in-Publication Data
Brighton, Catherine.
Mozart: scenes from the childhood of the great composer/
Catherine Brighton.
p.   cm.
Summary: A biography concentrating on the childhood experiences of
the great eighteenth-century composer.
1. Mozart, Wolfgang Amadeus, 1756–1791—Childhood and youth—
—Juvenile literature.   2. Composers—Austria—Biography—Juvenile
literature.   [1. Mozart, Wolfgang Amadeus, 1756–1791—Childhood and
youth.   2. Composers.]   I. Title.
ML3930.M9B7   1990
780′.92—dc20   89-49248   CIP   MN AC
[B]
ISBN 0-385-41537-0
ISBN 0-385-41538-9 (lib. bdg.)

MOZART

Scenes from the Childhood
of the Great Composer

Catherine Brighton

DOUBLEDAY
NEW YORK LONDON TORONTO SYDNEY AUCKLAND

SALZBURG

My name is Maria Anna Walburga Ignatia Mozart. My brother is Johannes Chrysostomus Wolfgangus Amadeus Mozart.

On ordinary days Mama and Papa call me Nannerl. They call my brother Wolferl but I call him Wolfi.

We lived in Salzburg and our Papa wrote music for Count Schrattenbach. Most mornings and every evening he went to the palace to work. In the afternoons Papa taught us music.

By the time I was nine I could play the clavier very well, but Wolfi soon caught up. When he was four he could accompany me on the clavier when I sang. When I played the clavier Wolfi joined me on his violin. He could learn a minuet and trio in half an hour.

PAPA'S PLAN

Papa made us practice very hard. We loved to play but sometimes we would have to start before breakfast. Wolfi had written some pretty pieces of music and Papa paced up and down the room, calling instructions.

"Fortissimo! Molto fortissimo!" he would shout, and our fingers ached as they beat on the keys.

One evening Papa pulled us to him, one on each knee.

"We are going on an adventure," he said. "We are going to travel across Europe, and my clever babies will show all the kings and queens just how beautifully they can play."

Wolfi looked at me with his eyes wide.

"You will be like royalty, and people will bow to you," laughed Papa.

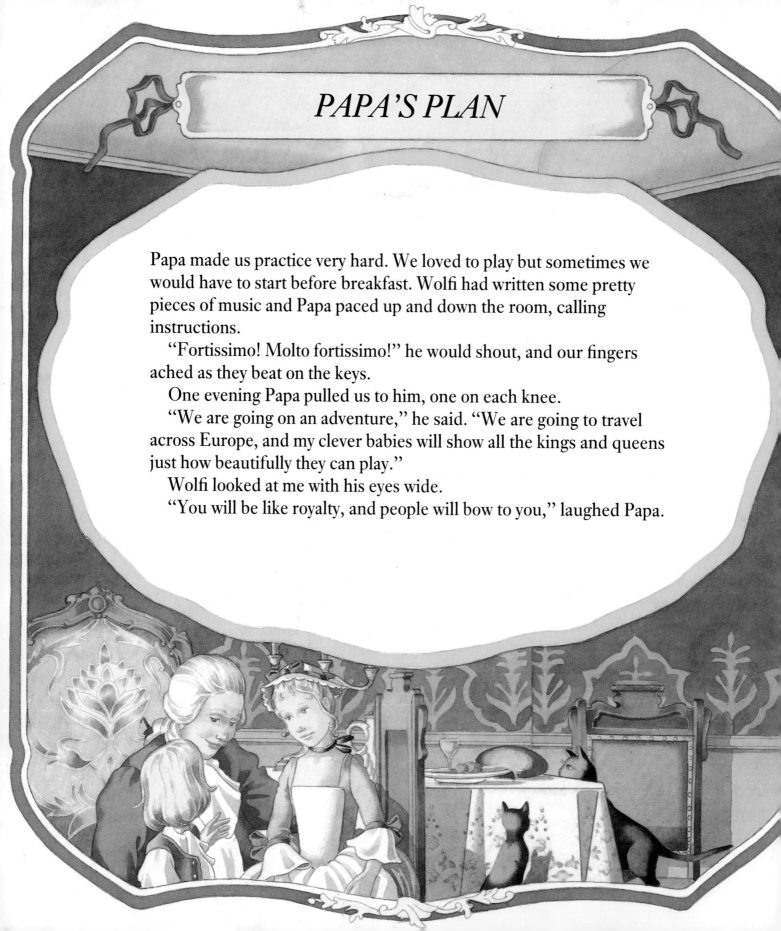

THE JOURNEY STARTS

Wolfi and I had never been on a boat before, but that was the way to get to Vienna. We said goodbye to Salzburg and Count Schrattenbach as our cases and trunks were loaded onto the boat.

We could see our faces gazing up at us from the smooth dark waters of the river Danube. The boat did not seem to move but the scenery glided past. There were castles high up on steep banks and in the distance we saw a flock of cranes fly silently by.

"How big is the world, Papa?" asked Wolfi, gazing at the mountains.

"Today your world is small, Wolferl, but one day it will be huge."

VIENNA

In Vienna Wolfi and I were taken to the Schönbrunn Palace where we met the Empress Maria Theresa. We played our very best for her and the courtiers clapped and cheered.

"They are the sweetest darlings I have ever heard play," said the Empress. "So much talent in such tiny bodies."

Everyone clapped again and I felt my face go hot and pink. The Empress's husband bent down and took Wolfi's hand.

"You're quite a little wizard, young man, but I bet you can't play with just one finger."

I think it was a joke, but Wolfi climbed back on the stool and played several pieces with one finger.

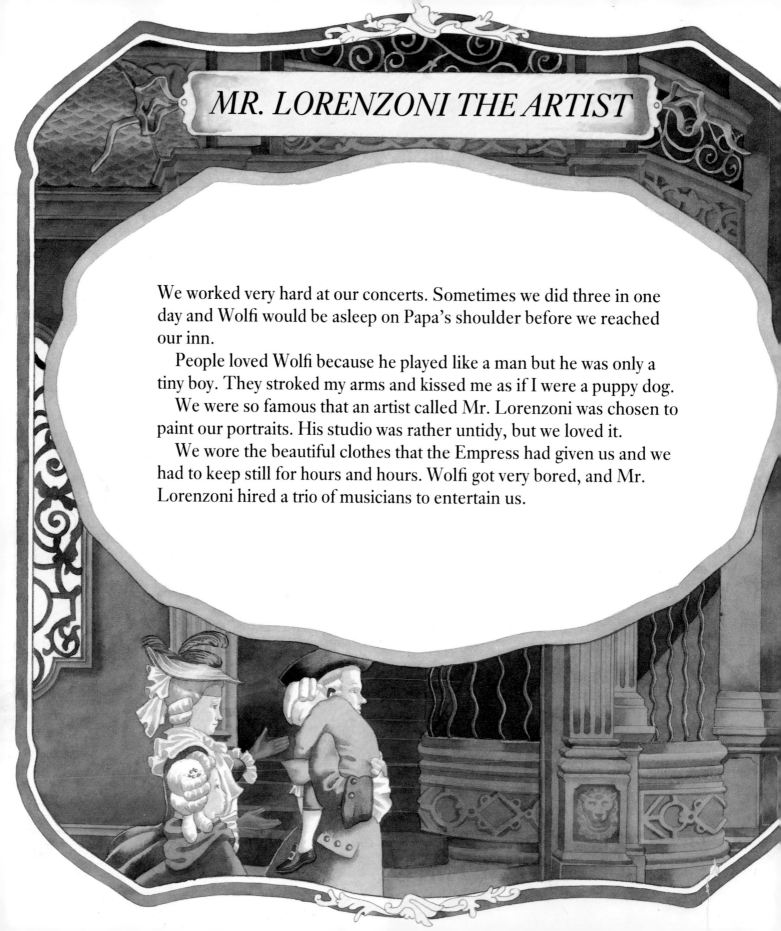

MR. LORENZONI THE ARTIST

We worked very hard at our concerts. Sometimes we did three in one day and Wolfi would be asleep on Papa's shoulder before we reached our inn.

People loved Wolfi because he played like a man but he was only a tiny boy. They stroked my arms and kissed me as if I were a puppy dog.

We were so famous that an artist called Mr. Lorenzoni was chosen to paint our portraits. His studio was rather untidy, but we loved it.

We wore the beautiful clothes that the Empress had given us and we had to keep still for hours and hours. Wolfi got very bored, and Mr. Lorenzoni hired a trio of musicians to entertain us.

PARIS

In Paris we met a very nice man called Melchior Grimm. Before we arrived he wrote about us and how we were so clever we could play with a blindfold around our eyes.

So when we gave our concert for the French King, a servant appeared and tied silk scarves around our eyes. Wolfi and I started to sulk.

"We're not performing monkeys, Wolfi," I whispered. "We're musicians."

But we knew Papa wanted us to play well, so our music was perfect and we saved our complaints for later. Papa was a bit cross.

"If you want people to hear your music you must do as they ask," he said, "especially when they are kings and queens."

Before I went to sleep I could see Wolfi sitting up in bed. He was composing music by the light of his candle.

THE ENGLISH CHANNEL

Wolfi and I were looking forward to going on the boat to England. We had loved the boat trip down the Danube—but the English Channel was a bit different! A very cold wind was blowing in our faces and the sky was dark.

Papa had hired a special boat so we would be comfortable. The sailors were tying all our luggage down with thick ropes and Wolfi and I saw the sailors laughing at us.

As soon as the boat was let loose from the dock it was tossed up to the top of one wave, and then thrown down to the bottom of the next. It went up and down, up and down, and after ten minutes Wolfi and I were hanging over the side being sick into the sea.

"Heave ho, my hearties!" sang the sailors as we clung to the edge. We cried for three and a half hours, until we reached England.

JOHANN CHRISTIAN BACH

In London we stayed in a place called Soho, where every day for two hours we entertained our visitors. They called Wolfi a miracle boy and a genius, and begged him to make up music for them.

One evening we performed a concert by the river Thames, and afterward a very important composer came to see us. His name was Johann Christian Bach. Wolfi sat on Mr. Bach's knee and together they played beautifully on the pianoforte. We talked for hours about music.

"Listen, Mr. Bach, listen!" cried Wolfi, and his fingers scampered through a piece he had written.

"Good," said Mr. Bach, "but what about doing it this way . . ."

And on it went. Wolfi was never happier than when he was talking about music with someone who knew more than he did.

CHELSEA

Alas, poor Papa became very ill and our concerts had to stop. We moved to Chelsea, a village by the river Thames, and Papa lay in a darkened room. From our windows we could see fields and churches and other fine buildings.

For seven weeks we could not practice our music for fear of upsetting Papa. But if the weather was warm Mama took us to the gardens and we played our violins under the elm trees.

In the evenings Wolfi and I sat at the big oak table and wrote music. It was then, when he was only nine, that Wolfi composed his first symphony.

WOLFI'S TEST

The next year we were even more famous, and everyone wanted to hear Wolfi's music. I was very proud of my brother and clapped the loudest when he took his bows.

But there were some people who were very jealous of him. They made up horrible stories. They said that Wolfi was a tiny man pretending to be a boy, or that Papa wrote his music, and he was a cheat.

At last, a friendly man called Daines Barrington, who was a lawyer and a musician, offered to test Wolfi to see who was right.

Mr. Barrington spent hours with Wolfi. Afterward, he said that when Wolfi was not playing music he was just like any other boy of nine—he even left the pianoforte to chase the cat across the room! When he gave Wolfi a very difficult piece of music he played it easily, as if he had written it himself. And last of all, Wolfi wrote a complicated piece of music before Mr. Barrington's very eyes.

That was the end of the horrible stories.

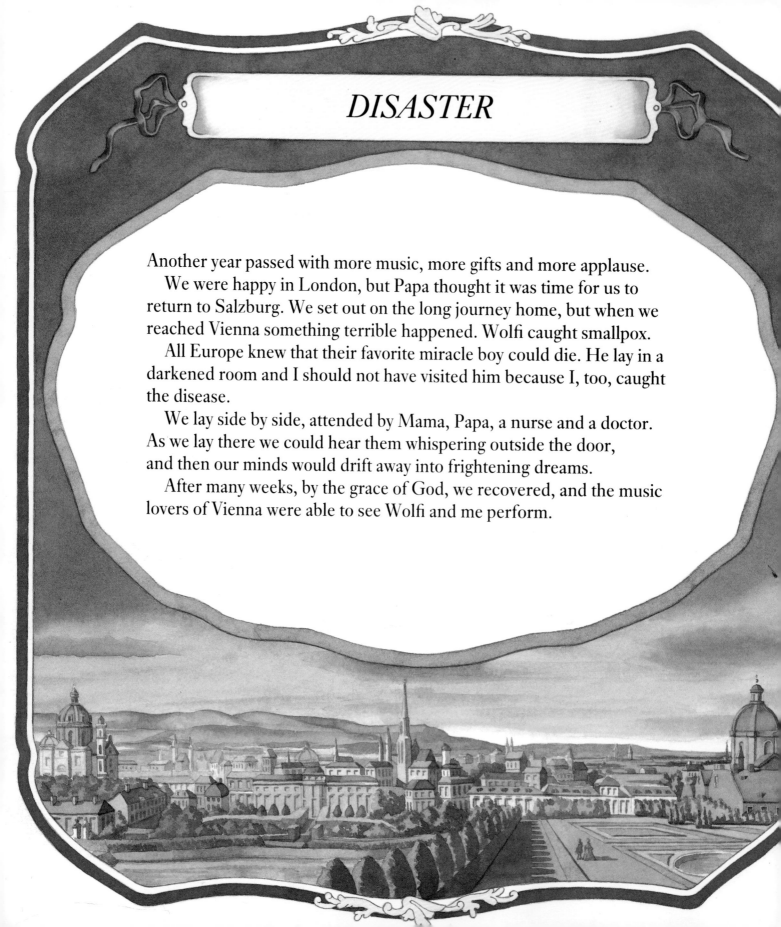

DISASTER

Another year passed with more music, more gifts and more applause.

We were happy in London, but Papa thought it was time for us to return to Salzburg. We set out on the long journey home, but when we reached Vienna something terrible happened. Wolfi caught smallpox.

All Europe knew that their favorite miracle boy could die. He lay in a darkened room and I should not have visited him because I, too, caught the disease.

We lay side by side, attended by Mama, Papa, a nurse and a doctor. As we lay there we could hear them whispering outside the door, and then our minds would drift away into frightening dreams.

After many weeks, by the grace of God, we recovered, and the music lovers of Vienna were able to see Wolfi and me perform.

WOLFI LEAVES

When I was sixteen I retired from the musical stage to become a teacher of the pianoforte. I was too old to be a miracle child, but Wolfi was now a famous composer although he was only eleven. Instead of always performing, he was writing operas for the Archbishop.

Papa decided to take him to Italy to see and hear Italian opera. So once again Wolfi packed his bags for the long journey.

But now, for the first time, he would be traveling without me.

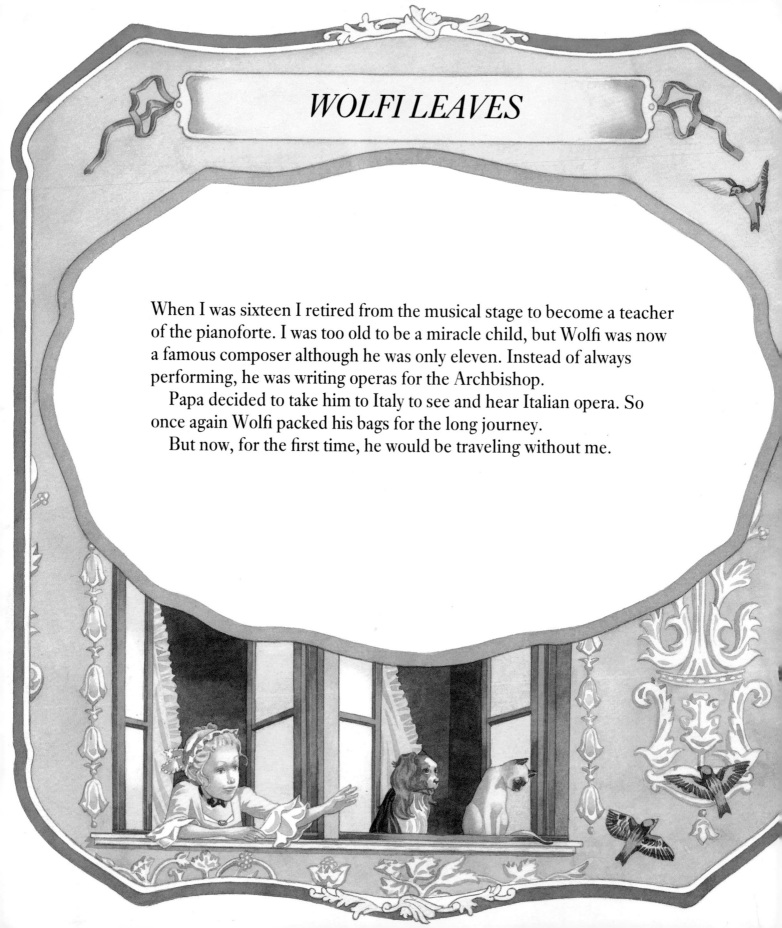

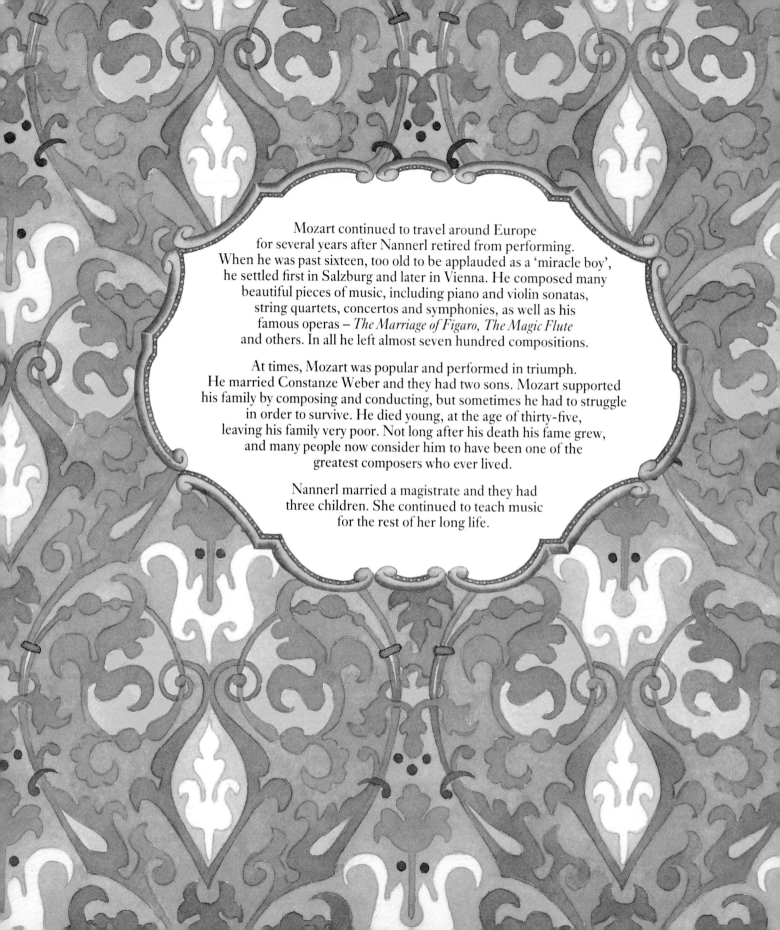

Mozart continued to travel around Europe
for several years after Nannerl retired from performing.
When he was past sixteen, too old to be applauded as a 'miracle boy',
he settled first in Salzburg and later in Vienna. He composed many
beautiful pieces of music, including piano and violin sonatas,
string quartets, concertos and symphonies, as well as his
famous operas – *The Marriage of Figaro, The Magic Flute*
and others. In all he left almost seven hundred compositions.

At times, Mozart was popular and performed in triumph.
He married Constanze Weber and they had two sons. Mozart supported
his family by composing and conducting, but sometimes he had to struggle
in order to survive. He died young, at the age of thirty-five,
leaving his family very poor. Not long after his death his fame grew,
and many people now consider him to have been one of the
greatest composers who ever lived.

Nannerl married a magistrate and they had
three children. She continued to teach music
for the rest of her long life.